Home Education

My First Year

A place to think and plan

Jacket design by Jamie Stewart.

ISBN: 9781089519034

What people are *saying* about this journal

66 *This is a delightful book I wish I'd had when I first began educating my children at home 18+ years ago. The pages are laid out in a manner that makes it easy to plan, reflect, and record not only what is working, but also what isn't.*

When one first begins to contemplate home education, it can be downright frightening. The options available can be overwhelming. This journal helps to negate this by helping the user think logically and systematically about the process. My favourite part, however, was the section for reflecting after the first year. I wish I had thought to do this not only after the first year, but after the fifth, tenth, and onward.

I believe this journal is beneficial to not only those families who are contemplating home education or have just begun, but also for families like myself who have been on this journey for years. It will make a wonderful keepsake to look back on. 99

Lisa Berry, US mother of three, home-schooling for 18 years

66 *This is a sorely needed introduction into home-ed life. Its simple and penetrative questions had me think clearly about problems, perspectives and goals. It cuts away, chapter by chapter, at the confusion and fear that can come with starting the first year. For over a decade, I experienced Dorothy treating home-education with realism and joy. Now I'm seeing her writing bring that realism and joy to an emerging generation.* 99

Jack Stewart, UK father of 3 young children, second generation home educator

" *This is not yet another 'how to' book but a journal to help guide you through the early stages of home education. The author presents each home education topic or concern, then gives the reader space to write out their own thoughts and make notes. While I'm now a veteran of home schooling, I remember feeling confused and a bit overwhelmed when I began to home educate. A journal such as this would have been a great help! I recommend this book to both new home educators and those considering home education.* "

Jodi Moore, US mother of four, home-schooling for 19 years

" *When I started homeschooling, I think I read every book on the market, and none of it would have been as valuable as this gem. This is a comprehensive journaling notebook that enables one to start a unique personalized homeschooling journey. It helps take information garnered and enables one to apply it to the everyday process and conflicts involved in homeschooling. The book is packed with journaling pages with prompts to tackle some of the unknowns.*

I found Dorothy's book to be wise and insightful. Most of the journal prompts were issues that I grappled with my first difficult year of homeschooling. It would have been very helpful to have a journal where I could collect all of my thought in one place. If I were to start my homeschooling journey all over again tomorrow, I would find this book to be an important process in my success as an educator. I know I will be handing a few copies of this journal to my friends who are just starting to embark on their new home-schooling journey. I am confident this will be a wonderful tool. "

Rachel Downs, US mother of five, home-schooling for 24 years

Dedicated to

My **husband**, Jamie Stewart
> who helps me do everything, including finding my glasses.

My **daughter**, Grace Stewart
> the guinea pig, who broke the rules about children
> and put up with all my educational experimentation.

My **son**, Jack Stewart
> who broke all the rules about children that Grace forgot to
> break (and did it with a smile).

My **grandchildren**, Janna, Nahum and Amos
> who are simply a delight.

Acknowledgements

Thank you to...

...my family for all their encouragement, particularly to Jack for reading an early draft, and Jamie for all his oversight of the design, editing and production process.

...Darcy Baldwin at DJB Fonts for the use of one of her creations for the titles.

...my home educating friends Carolyn Crawshaw, Margaret Haynes, Vivienne Sharkey and Christine Waterman, for reading this book and making valuable suggestions for improvements.

Welcome to your home education journey!

An exciting voyage of discovery awaits!

You are probably reading this book for one of two reasons, and I hope the process of completing it will help you in either case:

1. **Considering** home education

   You may be wondering whether this is the best decision for your child and want to do some preparatory thinking about it before taking the plunge. You may be the kind of person who likes all their ducks in a row.

2. **Just starting** home education

   You may already have made the decision to home educate your child and want to start gathering your thoughts, notes and plans in one place, helping you to develop a strategy or a home education philosophy.

I hope this journal will record your journey through your first year and that you will come back to it again and again as a place where you keep your collected information and developing ideas. I also hope that the journal will act as a caring friend, helping and prompting you to consider a few things you may not have thought about or just encouraging you along your path.

Dorothy Murphy
Summer 2019

Photo © Dorothy Murphy

How to use this book

The book is divided into four sections, which are designed to help you through the earlier stages of your home education journey:

Stage 1 - Deciding and Researching

Stage 2 - Preparing

Stage 3 - Planning

Stage 4 - Looking Back & Moving Forward

If your decision is already made, you may still find it beneficial to work through Stage 1 and think about the questions it raises. If you want to read through and make your notes in a linear way, because that is how you like to do things, that will work. If you are the kind of person who likes to jump around, doing things in your own way, that will work too, but keep Stage 4 until after you have been home-educating for a while. It is designed to help you evaluate your decisions and methods with a touch of hindsight.

The book can also be used as a record of your experiences, to remind you of your thinking (which may, of course, change with experience) and as a momento of your first year with your children as a home-educating family.

Notes

1. 'H.E.' is used throughout and, depending on the context, stands for 'home education', 'home educating' or other derivative.

2. 'Home Education' is the term used by parents in the UK who are educating their own children outside of a school setting. If you are American, you would be more familiar with the term 'home schooling'. For the purposes of this book, they are interchangeable.

3. 'Child' (singular) is used throughout, but please read as 'children' if that fits your situation.

Contents

Deciding *and* Researching

Is Home Education right for my family?

Photo © Dorothy Murphy

Your child is going to be central to your decision to home educate.

Describe
my child in 5 words

Name _____

Describe
my child in 5 words

Name _____

Describe
my child in 5 words

Name

Describe
my child in 5 words

Name

4

It can be helpful to write down the *reasons* you are considering H.E. Often there are both 'push' and 'pull' factors.

A **push** factor might be any difficulties a child is experiencing right now in school. A **pull** factor might be the freedom to arrange an education tailored to the needs of your individual child.

Write down as many push/ pull factors you can think of for H.E.

Push

Pull

My *concerns* about home education

Most parents had some concerns about H.E. before they started. Sometimes these worries turn out to be unfounded, so don't worry if you seem to have a lot of them. Write them down here, on the left hand side and leave space to update yourself as to whether your concerns turned out to be actual.

Concerns before I started H.E.	Still a problem? After...	
	1 month	6 months

concerns

	before I started H.E.	Still a problem? After...	
		1 month	6 months

Things we would be *free* to do in our own way

e.g. learning to read when my child is ready (not when the rest of the class is), or learning other languages intensively in the first few years.

Things we would be *free* to do in our own way

Things we might *miss* about taking the school route through education.

We might miss...	Ways to compensate?
e.g.	~ Joining a gym/ swim club or finding an H.E. sports group
~ School sports	~ Finding local H.E. families
~ School gate friendships	

We might *miss*	Ways to compensate?

Being *intentional* in our approach to H.E.

Some home educators find that they need to be slightly more intentional about a few things which school may have automatically sorted for them.

What might I need to be more intentional about?

What?	How can I deal with that?
e.g.	~ Contact doctor about any routine screening tests
~ Health screenings	~ Invite people to our home for play-dates
~ Making friends	

Being *intentional*

What?	How can I deal with that?

Online *information* about home education

There is an abundance of information and support out there in the home education community, both online and in groups of families meeting together on a regular basis.

Make notes here on **websites**, **blogs**, **social media** pages and **groups** which you find out about.

Online *support* I may find helpful

Make notes here on **websites**, **blogs**, **social media** pages and **groups** which you find out about.

Regular *local* groups I have discovered
(within one hour's travelling distance):

1

Where _____

When _____

Activity _____

Contact _____

Cost _____

2

_____

_____

_____

_____

_____

3

Where _____

When _____

Activity _____

Contact _____

Cost _____

4

_____

_____

_____

_____

_____

5

Where _____

When _____

Activity _____

Contact _____

Cost _____

6

_____

_____

_____

_____

_____

Regular *local* groups I have discovered
(within one hour's travelling distance):

1

Where _____

When _____

Activity _____

Contact _____

Cost _____

2

_____

_____

_____

_____

_____

3

Where _____

When _____

Activity _____

Contact _____

Cost _____

4

_____

_____

_____

_____

_____

5

Where _____

When _____

Activity _____

Contact _____

Cost _____

6

_____

_____

_____

_____

_____

Regular *non-local* groups
(further than one hour away):

1

Where   _____

When   _____

Activity   _____

Contact   _____

Cost   _____

2

_____

_____

_____

_____

_____

3

Where   _____

When   _____

Activity   _____

Contact   _____

Cost   _____

4

_____

_____

_____

_____

_____

5

Where   _____

When   _____

Activity   _____

Contact   _____

Cost   _____

6

_____

_____

_____

_____

_____

Regular *non-local* groups
(further than one hour away):

1

Where ....
When ....
Activity ....
Contact ....
Cost ....

2

....
....
....
....
....

3

Where ....
When ....
Activity ....
Contact ....
Cost ....

4

....
....
....
....
....

5

Where ....
When ....
Activity ....
Contact ....
Cost ....

6

....
....
....
....
....

What are the *advantages/ disadvantages* of the groups?

e.g. location, cost, type of activity, etc

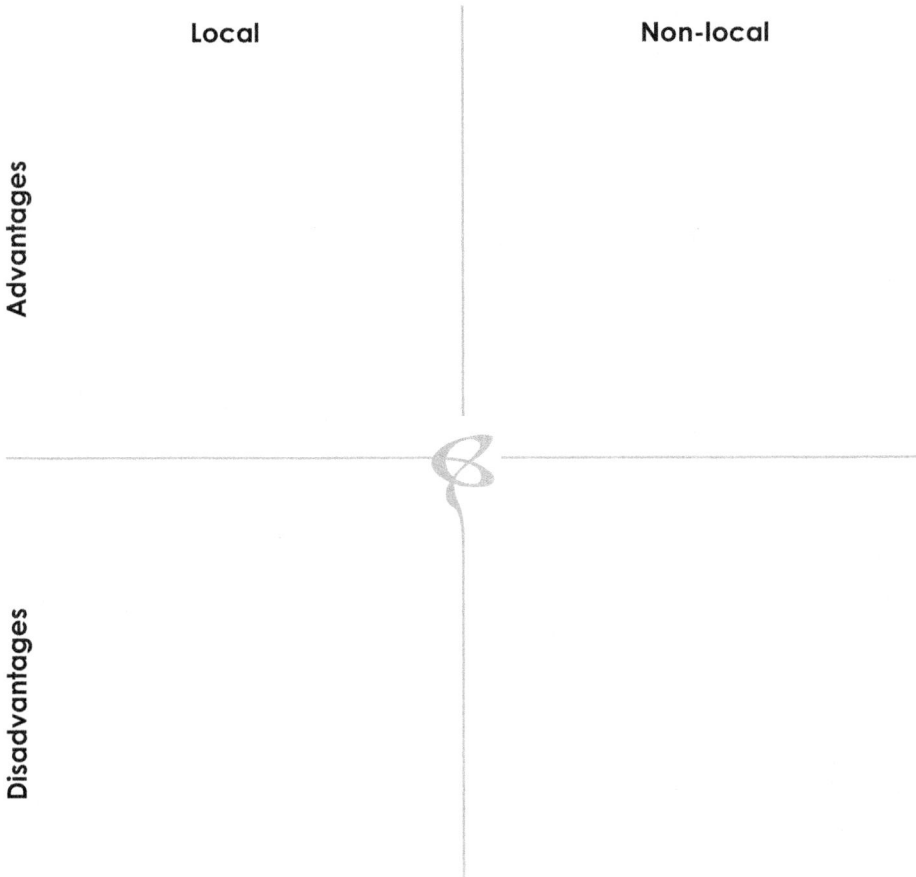

	Local	Non-local
Advantages		
Disadvantages		

Weighing up the choices, which shall I try to join and/ or try out first?

Why?

Support from friends and family

Who is likely to be our biggest supporter for our decision to home educate?

Whose support will I definitely need to make this work?

Can I enlist anyone else's support or help in this venture? Certain family members may relish the idea of being involved.

Where might I meet opposition to our plans?

How could I deal with such opposition?

When can I *schedule* chats with the people named?

Who	When	Outcome/ follow up

Educational *approaches* and *philosophies*

You may already have your own ideas about how you would like to home-educate. Or you may like to do some research on the different methods before deciding, *e.g. curriculum led, un-schooling, Charlotte Mason-inspired, Classical Education, etc*

Approaches I have researched already:

Approaches I have heard about and would like to find out more about:

My ideas at the moment:

As you are the expert when it comes to your child, is there an approach which you think might suit them best?

My child(ren) would like to:

The approach which might suit us best as a family:

Resources suited to our planned approach:

Am I ready to *decide* yet?

Now that you have begun to think things through, what other information do you need to help you make a decision to move forward?

What do I need to know?

Where can I go to have remaining questions answered?

Am I comfortable with leaving some questions unanswered?

Am I ready to decide?
My/ our decision to home-educate is (circle your choice):

yes   yes   no
                       but not yet

Preparing

Picture © Janna Stewart

Congratulations!

If you are at this page, then it looks like you've made the decision to home-educate your child(ren).

Support organisations

You may find it helpful to understand the law concerning H.E. in your country/ region. National support organisations and established H.E. websites will inform you of the process of withdrawal from school, and your rights and duties as a home-educating parent.

National support organisations:

1. _____

2. _____

3. _____

4. _____

The law says I can... _____

...and I need to... _____

On our *first day* what can I expect to happen?

This will be partly determined by how you have prepared for it.
What do **you** want to achieve on your first day?

Goals

1. _____
2. _____
3. _____
4. _____
5. _____
6. _____

What do the **children** want to happen on their first day?

Goals

1. _____
2. _____
3. _____
4. _____
5. _____
6. _____

Some people like to *celebrate* the first (and sometimes last) day of each academic year. Some families enjoy the marking of significant milestones.

How could we mark the **start** of the home-educating year?

e.g.

~ *special photo of each child*

~ *a local Not Back to School Picnic*

How could we celebrate the **end** of the home-educating year?

e.g.

~ *giving a special gift*

~ *going to a theme park with other home-educating families*

Siblings

Are you going to be home-educating two or more siblings? There are advantages and disadvantages to this. For example, sometimes siblings can learn the same things at the same time, making practicalities simpler. However, if their personalities, interest or ages diverge significantly, some extra effort and thought may need to go into planning how you do things as a family.

Home-educating siblings together

Advantages

Disadvantages

How might we need to approach this?

Finances - *income*

Make no mistake: home educating your child will have an impact on your finances. Firstly, someone will need to be home with your child, and that usually means that at least one parent will probably not be able to work full-time. Sometimes, families make things work with part-time work and/ or the help of grandparents, etc.

There will also be other costs involved; for example, you may spend more on heating your home in the winter because the children will be at home, not in school; there will be no free school meals. And there will be other budget implications, too.

What are the effects of H.E. on our household income?

What is our household income now?

Can we increase aspects of our income?

Who would work less/ give up their job in order to H.E.?

What would be the effect of that on our household income?

What can we do without/ sell?

Finances - *outgoings*

Many families start small and very frugally. A library card and access to a park can take you a long way towards meeting your child's needs. What you add to that, and when, will in part be determined by what you can afford.

Which of these do we want/ need?

e.g.
~ *Stationery supplies*
~ *Art & craft supplies*
~ *Books/ workbooks*
~ *Educational toys*
~ *IT equipment*
~ *Exam costs*
~ *Music tuition*
~ *Sports classes/ clubs*
~ *Visits to educational sites*
~ *Local H.E. group membership costs*
~ *Community group membership (e.g. Scouts)*
~ *An annual pass to a zoo or museum*

outgoings

What I can afford to buy **now**	What I may need **later**

More on H.E. *budgets*

There is no need to panic about expenditure. Some H.E. families trade skills with each other through local groups. H.E. families frequently work together to get 'school rate' discounts for things such as H.E. websites and visits to places of interest. Enterprising home educators have always found their own way round problems, e.g. some H.E. children learn an instrument and get excellent tuition through joining a local brass band. This is where involvement in a local community of H.E. families is essential, to pick up such tips.

What **skills/ equipment/ experiences** do I have which I could share with others in exchange for something we need?

What skills/ equipment/ experiences would I really like my children to have which I may not be able to supply myself?

How might we go about exchanging these things?

Basic equipment and *resources* for young children

There is nothing you really need, aside from pencils, pens and paper, to start with, especially with young children. However, a few of the following will be helpful.

Things to develop...

- fine motor skills
    e.g. threading toys, scissors, pencils

- gross motor skills
    e.g. tricycle, skates, bike, scooter

- creativity
    e.g. painting materials, home-made playdough, junk modelling stuff

- hand/ eye coordination
    e.g. bats & balls, construction sets

- imaginative play
    e.g. dressing-up clothes, dolls and natural objects such as shells, stones, sticks, etc

- language development
    e.g. picture books

You can build up your collection of useful things gradually, using charity shops (thrift stores), etc. And make use of your local library.

resources

I have

I would like

A *place* for everything

All the resources you start to collect will need arranging or it will engulf you! Bookcases and storage boxes might help.

Places to keep our stuff:

Books

Play equipment

Science equipment

Crafts

Completed crafts!

Music, sports, etc.

Most families have an abundance of these things, but H.E. families usually have more than most! If space is at a premium at your house, this may need thinking about.

Special circumstances

Families home educate in hugely varied circumstances. Few situations make it impossible. There are online support groups for just about every circumstance you can think of, such as single parents, parents of children with Special Educational Needs or Disabilities (SENDs), etc.

Picture © Nahum Stewart

Recovering from difficult *school* experiences

You may have found yourself home-educating in order to rescue your child from a negative or traumatic school experience. Plenty of families find themselves in that situation. There is sometimes a sense of urgency about getting started, especially with an older child, before researching H.E. properly. The problem is that you can make some costly mistakes, e.g. by buying expensive curricula which is unsuitable for your child, if you allow yourself to be panicked into starting at full speed straight away.

If your child has been bullied or experienced any kind of trauma at school, you may find that there is some understandable resistance to trying to replicate school at home. In any case, your child may need time to deal with the things that have happened and to recover. Sometimes, this process of recovery is called *deschooling*. Try to get in touch with other local home educators, and consider and plan before starting.

Does my child need recovery time? How much?

Special circumstances - *special needs*

Sometimes parents begin to home-educate because they know
or suspect that their child has a special need and would benefit
from being educated differently than in school. If this is you, you are
certainly not alone. If your child is enrolled at a special school, or has
an EHCP (or ILP in the US) in place, you have more to consider.

What benefits are there to home-educating my child? _____
*e.g. taking time to lay strong foundations in basic skills before moving
on.*

What possible problems might we encounter? _____
e.g. need for Access Arrangements in public examinations

What might I need to take personal responsibility for, which school
may have done as part of its responsibility? _____
e.g. organise speech therapy

Special circumstances - *teens*

Perhaps your teenager is about to begin, or has already embarked on, exam courses. There is no 'alternative system' for doing this, and it will take organising on your part, but don't worry - plenty of home-educating families have helped their children to achieve qualifications, or to circumvent them through such things as apprenticeships.

Subjects my teen would like to study:

1. _____
2. _____
3. _____
4. _____
5. _____
6. _____
7. _____
8. _____
9. _____
10. _____

(Many home educated teens sit fewer exams than 10 though. Don't feel the need to fill in all the gaps!)

There are lots of ways, both traditional and non-traditional, to move forward through education in the teen years. Try to explore all of them before making a decision, checking that your information is completely up-to-date.

Special circumstances - *large family*

There is a long tradition of large families in the home-education community and you are definitely not going to be unusual. You could search for some blogs to inspire you.

What will be the main benefits of home-educating a large family?

What is going to be my trickiest 'large family' issue with H.E. and what steps can I take to help with that?

Which child (if any) in the family might need more of my attention at the moment?

Special circumstances - *single parent*

There are single parents who have chosen to home-educate their child(ren). It is definitely possible. You might find it helpful to find a support group as soon as you can.

Many things you will need to take into account are the same as for other parents but one that is different is how much the child(ren)'s other parent has to contribute to the decision about how their child is educated. Obviously, things will be much easier if they are also in favour of home-education.

What are my **rights** regarding education in my specific situation?

What are my **responsibilities**?

Special circumstances - *single parent*

What can I do to help the process of H.E. go smoothly?

What are the potential problems I might encounter?

Who can I go to for information and/ or support?

Special circumstances - *adoption & fostering*

Many home-educating families who adopt children find that H.E. works well for them, but others decide that school is the best option. If you decide to H.E., then make sure that you find support for that decision.

What are my **rights** regarding H.E. in a fostering and/ or adoption situation?

Are there any specific **issues** regarding H.E. in these circumstances I need to research more?

Support groups for H.E. adopters I have found

When *Dad* is the main home educator

At this time, most H.E. groups tend to be full of mothers and their children, although spotting a father in these groups has become more common in recent years. You may not find this a problem at all! Or you may find it throws up challenges for your family.

Are there any issues I can foresee with being a home-educating father?

How can I address them?

Support I have found for this role.
e.g. groups, podcasts, websites, blogs

Home educating a *single child*

When you are home-educating one child, either because their siblings are at school or you only have one child, your circumstances may mean you have to adopt a different approach. For example, you may find yourself much more directly involved as your child's playmate. When you think this through, will this be a problem? Maybe not!

Will my child need more of my time and involvement?
Am I happy to meet those needs?

How can my child's needs for regular interaction with other children be met?

Stage

3

Planning

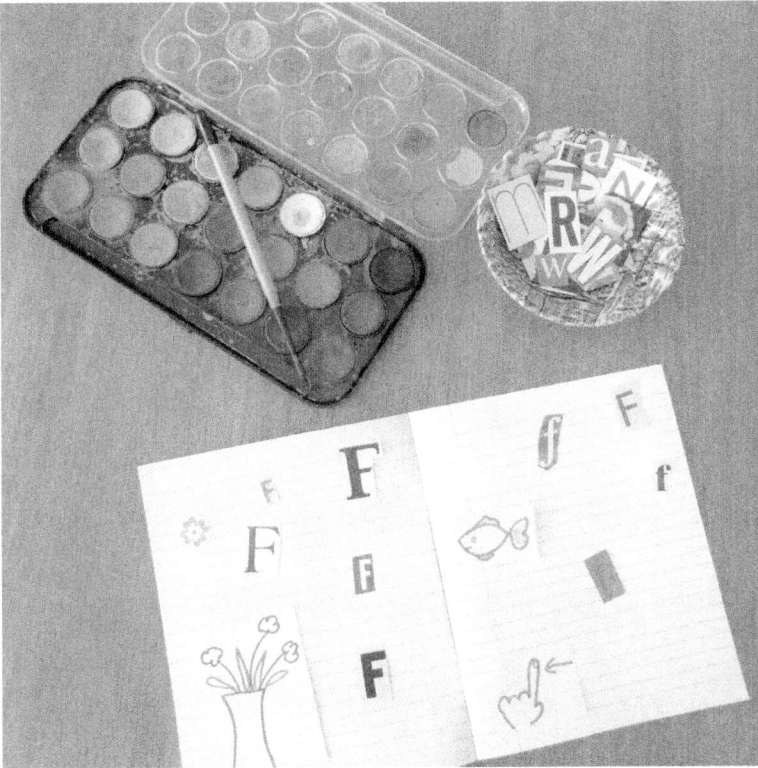

Photo © Dorothy Murphy

A word about bought *curricula*

There are some great ones out there. Some are freely available online. Some are bought with everything you need in one box. Each has its own philosophy, flavour and purpose, and is one way to meet your child's or your family's needs.

However, such curricula don't suit everyone! Some families don't use any pre-designed curricula. Some like to design their own, so that they are perfectly tailored to their child's needs. Many like to pick and mix elements of one, elements of another and create other elements for themselves. Some families just want someone else to do all the curriculum planning for them, and are happy to pay for that service. There is no right or wrong way for your family.

One thing might be helpful to remember, though: any curriculum is designed to be a servant, not a master. It's there to work for you, not to dominate and oppress you.

Curricula I have seen which could be helpful:

Routines, patterns and rhythms - part 1

You will probably find that your family settles into a pattern for the days and weeks which suits you. It may not look like the pattern that other families enjoy, but that is the beauty of home education, that it's personal to you.

If you are a person who dislikes routines and timetables and have left the school system behind, at least in part because you wanted to be free of them, then it may take you longer to establish a pattern for your days which works for you because you are experimenting with a different way of life.

Try thinking of the days as having a helpful rhythm, rather than a timetable with deadlines. Slow down, breathe, discover how you and your children function, grow and thrive best, and then develop a rhythm together.

How do I feel about our daily rhythms now?

How do the children feel about our daily rhythms?

Educational *goals* for the **first year**

Are there goals you would like to achieve for your child in the first year? Does the child have a goal? Can you think of a route through to achieving them?

Child's name:

What is my child like now? What can they do?
e.g. very sociable, enjoys new situations, makes friends easily

What goals would **I** like them to achieve in the next year?
e.g.
~ *grow in confidence with maths*
~ *be happier/ less stressed*

What are my **child**'s goals for the next year?
e.g. wants to
~ *learn how to make things out of wood*
~ *learn French*

Educational *goals* for the **first year**

Child's name:

What is my child like now? What can they do?

What goals would **I** like them to achieve in the next year?

What are my **child**'s goals for the next year?

Educational *goals* for the **first year**

Child's name: _____

What is my child like now? What can they do?

What goals would **I** like them to achieve in the next year?

What are my **child**'s goals for the next year?

Educational *goals* for the **first year**

Child's name:

What is my child like now? What can they do?

What goals would **I** like them to achieve in the next year?

What are my **child**'s goals for the next year?

Educational *goals* by the **end of their education**

What kind of person are you hoping your child will be by the time they have grown up? What qualities would you like for your grown-up child? The answer to this, more than anything else, will shape your educational philosophy.

Child's name:

Qualities - *e.g. kind, confident, excited about learning*	How can I help them develop those qualities?

Educational *goals* by the **end of their education**

Child's name: _____

Qualities - *e.g. kind, confident, excited about learning*	How can I help them develop those qualities?

Educational *goals* by the **end of their education**

Child's name: _____

Qualities - *e.g. kind, confident, excited about learning*	How can I help them develop those qualities?

Educational *goals* by the **end of their education**

Child's name:

Qualities - *e.g. kind, confident, excited about learning*	How can I help them develop those qualities?

Family learning *goals*

You have a wonderful opportunity to develop learning as a family.
What would your family like to learn about together?
*e.g. family/ local history, learning and playing instruments together,
participating in a sport as a family.*

Goals for our family learning	How can we achieve this?

Family learning *goals*

Goals for our family learning	How can we achieve this?

Children's learning *goals*

You might like to ask each child what they would like to learn about first. Perhaps someone is desperate to learn to read, or to find out about animals, or volcanoes, or would like to ride a bike so they can go for adventures with you, or paint, or play tennis, or speak Swahili, or do quadratic equations, or astronomy!

Perhaps they have never been asked this before: "What would you like to learn?"

Child:

Goals:

Child:

Goals:

Children's learning *goals*

Child:

Goals:

Child:

Goals:

Child:

Goals:

86

When your child has *no goals*

Sometimes, children who have been to school are temporarily unable to set their own goals. Sometimes, they can find the question "What would you like to learn?" unanswerable.

Are there ways you can help such a child to move forward in a positive way?

Pace yourself or burn out!

It's not a race, and it's not a competition!

At the start of your home education experience, it's vital to set a sustainable pace for you and your child(ren). If you try to pack too much into your week, you may end up burning out and giving up. Think about the kind of personalities you have in your family, how easily you get stressed, and balance that against too little pace and boredom.

Many families find they benefit from a slow start, just enjoying each other's company for a while, and learning to live with each other's quirks full-time. If your child is recovering from a difficult school experience, you may well need a period of 'deschooling'.

Other families love to get stuck right in, going to H.E. groups, socialising with other H.E. children, choosing topics to learn about, etc. There is no wrong way to H.E., so finding the right pace depends entirely on your own circumstances.

My thoughts on pacing:

Planning

Some home educators like to plan far ahead, years even, especially if they have teens who are working towards a specific goal. Others like things to be really loose and ultra-flexible. There is no right and wrong here, only what is best for your family.

You might like to experiment with daily, weekly or termly plans. Example frameworks for each follow.

Daily Plan Example

	Jane (6)	David (12)	Amy (14)
Morning:	Reading - Frog & Toad	Maths & spelling	Maths & spelling
	Science experiments - water		
	Help me make lunch	History - read p48 - 53	English essay
Lunch:	Brown family here for lunch & play		
After-noon:	Learn to knit	Skype Economics lesson	To Zayla's house for book group
Evening:	Brownies 6pm	Making pizza for us	Dad pick up 7pm

Planning

Weekly Plan Example - David (12)

Mon   *Maths, spelling, History reading, Economics by Skype (with tutor)*

Tue   *Economics homework, Maths, English Literature reading*

Wed   *Swimming class, lunch out, reading*

Thur   *Home Ed group in town, Science study*

Fri   *English Literature essay, play rehearsal with Drama group*

Notes   *Check dates English Literature homework due*

Termly Plan Example - Jane (6)

~ *She wants to learn to knit!*
~ *Progress with reading - aim to read 4 beginner books unaided by end of term*
~ *Lots of painting and drawing practice*
~ *Go for weekly nature walks with friends*
~ *Have one friend from Brownies/ H.E. group over for lunch, once a month*
~ *Go to Legoland workshops with H.E. group*
~ *Visit Natural History Museum in Oxford*
~ *Buy her a recorder*
~ *Keep going with speech therapy!*

Planning

Want to try some out?

Day

Morning:

Lunch:

Afternoon:

Evening:

Notes:

Planning

Day

Morning:

Lunch:

Afternoon:

Evening:

Notes:

Planning

	Day

Morning:

Lunch:

Afternoon:

Evening:

Notes:

Planning

Day

Morning:

Lunch:

Afternoon:

Evening:

Notes:

Planning

Week

Mon

Tue

Wed

Thur

Fri

Notes:

Week

Mon

Tue

Wed

Thur

Fri

Notes:

Planning

Week _____

Mon

Tue

Wed

Thur

Fri

Notes

Week _____

Mon

Tue

Wed

Thur

Fri

Notes

Planning

Term

Notes:

Term

Notes:

Planning

Term

Notes:

Term

Notes:

Planning *downtime*

Some families find themselves getting over-scheduled. If this happens, you could just use your plan to build in some downtime - time when you don't have to go anywhere and the children can just rest, day-dream and play. These activities are just as important as studying, socialising and experiencing educational outings. Most families find the balance that's right for them after a while.

Our favourite rest days:

Educational *philosophies*

You may have found out about several different educational philosophies by now, and are wondering which one would suit your family the best. Keep some notes on a few of them here.

1

2

3

4

Books to read

You have probably come across the titles of some books about H.E. that look interesting. Keep a list of such titles here.

Books I would like to read	Found/ bought	Read

Educational *visits* / field *trips*

One of the best parts of H.E.!

Can't wait to get out there and learn with your children? What are the visits you are most excited to do? Which ones are the children most excited about?

Trips/ visits we would like to take	When taken	Who liked it best?

Trips/ visits we would like to take	When taken	Who liked it best?

Trips/ visits we would like to take	When taken	Who liked it best?

Quotations about education

Quotation	Who said it?

Looking Back & Moving Forward

Photo © Dorothy Murphy

Piecing it all *together* (like a patchwork quilt)

My developing educational philosophy

$\mathcal{Time}$ management

Some of us run into problems organising and managing our time while home educating. Others don't!

How did I expect a typical day to look, before I started H.E.?

How does it actually look 3 months down the line?

What needs tweaking?

School *holidays* (or not)

"Do you take a break for school holidays?" is a common question asked of home educators. Different families do things in different ways, including

~ sticking to term time because (for example) one child in the family is going to school
~ keeping usual rhythms going all year round
~ remaining as flexible as possible in order to take advantage of any opportunities that come up.

If one parent has a '2 weeks at work + 1 week off' type of job, the beauty of H.E. is that you can do that too, if you like!

If you are following a structured approach, or curriculum, you may find that, after a long summer break, it is harder to get started again.

It might be easiest to have a sliding start, where you add in one extra element/ subject a day, until you are all back up to full steam!

My thoughts about our learning rhythm/ pattern:

Works for me!

As your family starts its H.E. journey, you will probably find a few things you try will fail miserably, or go down like a lead balloon with the kids. Don't panic! This will just help you all develop creativity! Soon, you will figure out the things that work well for you!

Make a note of what a **really good day** actually looked like. You can look back on this after a bad day. It may help!

A **good day** home-educating!

What happened?

Lessons learned?

Anything repeatable?

Oops!

Everyone has **bad days**, like when you are stressed, the kids are sick, the washing machine has broken down and you are washing sheets and towels by walking up and down on them in a bath full of water, when the doorbell rings...

Wait! Was that only me??

A **bad day** home-educating!

What happened?

Lessons learned?

What not to repeat!

Refresh

Parents need to refresh themselves from time to time. Some need time away from the constant 24/7 H.E. lifestyle. Others find refreshment in the company of other families at a H.E. gathering. You are allowed to attend to your own needs! Self-care is important and it teaches children a valuable life-lesson.

How are you likely to be able to meet your own self-care needs?
~   Ask relatives to help out occasionally/ regularly?
~   Time away in the evening when your partner is home?
~   Time-swap with another parent?
~   Paid-for childcare?
~   Building into the day a meaningful moment or treat to enjoy?

Other ideas?

Avoiding *burnout*

Some of us are slow to get going. Others of us hurtle through life trying to do everything all at once. The Hurtlers among us are prone to burnout. It **does not** mean that you have to ditch H.E., though.

It's not that it's not working. It may just require a change of approach. It's best to avoid burnout through careful consideration and regular reflection, but if you hit the burnout stage, try to stop, step away from your regular patterns, perhaps taking a family sabbatical for a week/ month/ term/ year. Relax, have some fun, be gentle with yourself and then re-evaluate what you were doing that caused the problems in the first place.

What can I do...
...to **avoid** burnout?

...to **recover** from burnout?

Record keeping

Your country/ state may have certain expectations regarding record-keeping, so it is important that you know what they are and keep up with any changes in regulations.

Some ways in which families can keep a record of their children's education can also prove to be a way of preserving delightful familiy memories, such as blogs, social media pages, photograph albums and journals. Some children like to keep a record of the books they are reading and the trips they go on. These can be very enjoyable to look back on in years to come.

What do we need to do to comply with the law regarding record keeping (if anything)?

How might we enjoy keeping a record of our educational journey?

Routines, patterns and rhythms - part 2

Have another read of Part 1 (page 73).

Have your daily and weekly rhythms settled into a pattern yet? You have probably found that they revolve around some enjoyable group events you participate in.

Our current **daily** rhythms

Our current **weekly** rhythms

Self-*evaluation*

It is true that not everyone is cut out for H.E. We are each unique individuals, so why would there not be variation in that?

Some seem born for it and sustain it for years with enthusiasm and panache. Others try it for a short while and feel they have made a big mess of the whole thing and everyone is happier when the children go back to school.

And there is every situation in between; you could H.E. only for primary or only for exam years. You could H.E. only the child with an SEND and not the others (or the other way round!) The important thing is to do what you think is right for your family.

No matter what your intentions are when you start, it may help if you do a bit of evaluation at intervals, asking yourself a few questions. Like these, perhaps:

~ Why are we still doing this?
~ Have we achieved our original intentions?
~ How can I make the experience better for us?
~ Do I need help with anything?
~ Would things be better if we stopped? How?
~ Would things be worse if we stopped? How?
~ Do we all want to continue? Why?

Self- *evaluation*

After the 1st **day**:

My thoughts

Children's comments

Self-*evaluation*

After the 1st **week**:

My thoughts

Children's comments

Self-*evaluation*

After the 1st **term**:

My thoughts

Children's comments

Self- *evaluation*

After the 1st **year**:

My thoughts

Children's comments

All *change*

Just when you have established a way of doing things, everything changes! The toddler gives up his afternoon nap; the older kids start to go to sleep later; someone seems to need a lot more 1:1 with you than before; an exam is on the horizon; a new baby is coming; someone is ill; a house move...

Nothing is permanent in H.E., as in life, so there is always a need to embrace change, or at least to try not to resist and resent it!

Changes we've noticed this year	How did we adapt to cope?

Changes we're anticipating next year	How can we adapt to cope?

Ups and downs

Just as there are seasons in life, they are also there in the home education journey. There may be periods of financial or relationship struggle, or of illness in the family, for example. We may need to adjust our course during these seasons.

It will help if we know that they may well happen and give ourselves permission to slow down, accept help or change direction.

Having to make these changes **does not** mean that we have failed as a parent or a home educator. It just means we are human. Other home educators will also have experienced these seasons. They may well have helpful information and suggestions for you.

How might I react to some unforeseen life-event?

How could I soften the effects on the children?

Could we keep home-educating?

Concerns revisited

Remember the concerns you had before starting to home-educate?
Look back to page 7 now. Are they still an issue?

Any continuing concerns and how I can deal with them

Pioneers, travellers and settlers

Every movement needs its pioneers, travellers and settlers.

Pioneers...
- ~ start groups
- ~ organise events
- ~ do things no one else has thought of
- ~ even enjoy the excitement of fresh challenges.

Travellers...
- ~ assist and encourage the pioneers
- ~ may tweak the way things are done
- ~ improve methods.

Settlers...
- ~ enjoy a pre-planned route
- ~ like to get involved in groups which already exist
- ~ may really value a settled community.

Are there aspects of one or more of these in your personality?
Is one of them more dominant?

Is there more you feel ready to do as part of the H.E. community?

The *first year*

You have just done something...
- ~ different
- ~ counter-cultural
- ~ challenging
- ~ incredibly worthwhile!

You have just completed your first year of home-education. You have taken the time to reflect on it and have evaluated the effects on your family.

Congratulations!

Time to plan for next year?

Advice from H.E. parents who have completed their journey

> " Remember to enjoy every day you have with your children. It will be over before you realise it. Carpe Diem! "

> " Never say 'never'! Don't trap yourself into a method, a philosophy, a curriculum. Allow your thinking to evolve with experience and with each child. "

> " Home education is a life-style, a whole family adventure, which can be gloriously fun if you embrace it. I resisted that for a long time, thinking of it as simply an alternative educational method. It's easier when you think of it as setting your children up for a lifetime of learning. "

> " Ask the veterans for advice! The H.E. community is so helpful. Leverage their experience. "

> " Your child is an individual. Try to tailor their education to their needs, rather than anyone's system. "

About *the author*

Dorothy Murphy is the mother of two home educated children, one of whom came home from school one day aged five and never went back. The other didn't even start school. They are both now thoroughly educated adults. She is also the grandmother of three home educated children.

Dorothy is a qualified and experienced secondary teacher and the SENDCO for a home educator-run exam centre. She delights in teaching and enjoys helping home educated teenagers through the UK state exam system.

She has a passion for child-centred education and has a strong interest in developing and protecting the parent-child relationship.

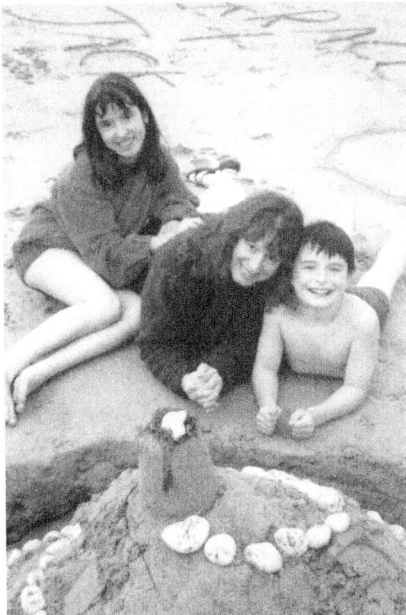

What little free time she has Dorothy devotes to the cultivation of community, the crafting of poems and the singing of songs.

151

Printed by Amazon Italia Logistica S.r.l.
Torrazza Piemonte (TO), Italy